**Amazing Planet Earth**

# EARTHQUAKES AND TSUNAMIS

## TERRY JENNINGS

$A^+$

**Smart Apple Media**

Smart Apple Media
P.O. Box 3263
Mankato, MN 56002

Printed in the United States of America

Library of Congress Cataloging-in-Publication Data

Jennings, Terry J.
  Earthquakes and tsunamis / Terry Jennings.
      p. cm. -- (Amazing planet earth)
  Includes index.
  ISBN 978-1-59920-372-0 (hardcover)
  1. Earthquakes--Juvenile literature. 2. Tsunamis--Juvenile literature. I. Title.
  QE521.3.J43 2010
  551.22--dc22
                        2008055496


Created by Q2AMedia
Editor: Katie Dicker
Art Director: Rahul Dhiman
Designer: Harleen Mehta
Picture Researcher: Shreya Sharma
Line Artist: Sibi N. Devasia
Coloring Artists: Indrim Boo, Mahender Kumar

All words in **bold** can be found in the glossary on pages 30–31.

Picture credits
t=top b=bottom c=center l=left r=right
CoverImage: pestanarui/ iStockphoto.
Back Cover Image: Robert Kaufmann/FEMA

Insides: U.S. Geological Survey: Title Page, Ben Simmons/ Photononstop/ Photolibrary: 4-5, Xiao Li/ EPA: 5b , Anjum Naveed/
Associated Press: 6, David Guttenfelder/ Associated Press: 7, Goran Tomasevic/ Reuters: 8, B.K.Bangash/ Associated Press: 9, National
Geophysical Data center/ NOAA: 11, U.S. Geological Survey: 12, U.S. Geological Survey: 13, U.S. Geological Survey: 15,Associated
Press: 16, Enric Marti/ Associated Press: 17, Kontos Yannis/ Corbis Sygma: 18, Enric Marti/ Associated Press: 19, Fouquin/
shutterstock: 20, Richard Vogel /Associated Press: 21, Earth Observatory/ NASA: 22, Eugene Hoshiko/ Associated Press: 23, NOAA:
25, Andy Z/ Shutterstock: 26, Svetlana Privezentsev/ Shutterstock: 26-27, Christophe Testi/ Shutterstock: 28, Diana Bier Torre Mayor /
Alamy: 29, Fouquin/ shutterstock: 31.

Q2AMedia Art Bank: 10, 11, 14, 24.


9 8 7 6 5 4 3 2 1

# Contents

# Violent Earthquakes

A powerful **earthquake** is one of the most frightening forces on Earth. When Earth's surface wobbles, it seems we no longer live on solid ground.

## Relieving Stress

Earthquakes are nature's way of relieving stress—more than 3 million of them affect Earth every year. Earthquakes also occur under the oceans and cause giant waves that are called a **tsunami**. Large earthquakes can be felt over thousands of miles, but fortunately, most earthquakes are very weak. Usually, they are only detected with delicate instruments.

The damages caused by an earthquake can range from the collapse of buildings to huge cracks in roads like this.

# Deadly Quakes

Powerful earthquakes occur without warning and can be strong enough to shake a city to the ground. Although it is possible to say where an earthquake is likely to occur, it is not possible to say when. In the last 100 years, more than 1.5 million people have died as a result of earthquakes. The effect on the survivors is immense. Billions of people have lost their homes and their loved ones. Schools and businesses have been destroyed, and livelihoods have been ruined.

## DATA FILE

- Earthquakes occur all over the world, but certain regions are particularly prone to them.

- The longest recorded earthquake, in Indonesia in 2004, lasted 10 minutes.

- Just before an earthquake, dogs are said to howl, rats and mice flee from their burrows, and fish thrash about in ponds.

- The deadliest earthquake was probably in Shaanxi, China, in 1556. It is believed to have killed more than 830,000 people.

● The survivors of China's Sichuan Province earthquake in 2008 were lucky to be alive, but faced injury, homelessness, and unemployment.

# Deadly Destruction

A powerful earthquake struck northern Pakistan and neighboring parts of India and Afghanistan in October 2005. It was the strongest—and deadliest—earthquake to affect the area in more than 100 years.

**Date:** October 2005
**Location:** Pakistan, India, Afghanistan
**Strength:** 7.6 on the Richter scale
**Fatalities:** Over 87,000

## Predawn Earthquake

The early morning of October 8, 2005, seemed like any other morning to the people living in the mountainous areas of northern Pakistan, northern India, and Afghanistan. Most students in Pakistan were at school. Without warning, disaster struck. There was a massive earthquake, measuring 7.6 on the **Richter scale**, about 16 miles (26 km) below the surface. It occurred at the point where Earth's **plate** carrying the Indian **subcontinent** moves toward the plate carrying Eurasia (see page 11). In comparison to other earthquakes, it was quite near to Earth's surface. The **vibrations** caused much damage.

• This block of apartments collapsed during the Pakistan earthquake of 2005.

## Casualties

Many children were buried as school buildings collapsed. Adults were trapped in their homes. Entire towns and villages were wiped out. In Islamabad, the capital of Pakistan, a 10-story building collapsed, killing most of its inhabitants. Throughout Pakistan and parts of India and Afghanistan, more than 87,000 people were killed and 75,000 were injured. An estimated 4 million people in the region were left homeless. By October 27, more than 1,000 **aftershocks** had been recorded. They continued for many more weeks.

## News Flash

### October 10, 2005

Pakistan's president has appealed for international help. His country cannot deal with the aftermath of the massive earthquake on its own.

More than 19,000 people are thought to have been killed in Pakistan, and it is feared the toll could rise much higher.

• After the Pakistan earthquake, local residents carried out rescue attempts. Aid organizations could not reach the scene because the roads were blocked.

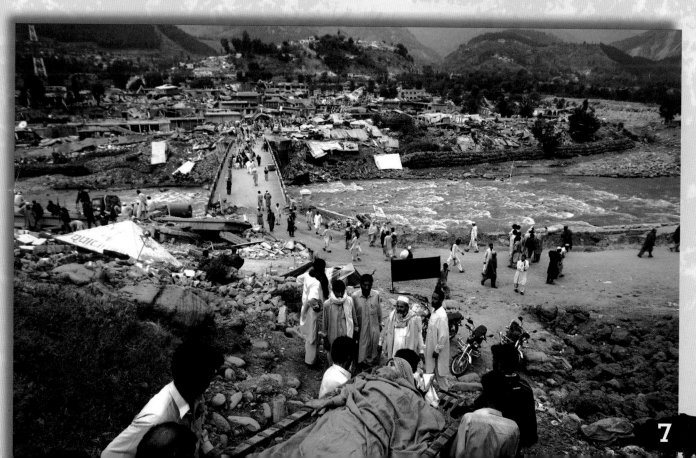

# The Aftermath

The next day, stunned survivors of the earthquake, many covered in blood, were camped out in the streets. They were afraid to return home because of the powerful aftershocks. As news of the worst disaster in Pakistan's history spread around the world, rescue workers prepared to go to the affected area. But **landslides** and rockfalls had destroyed the narrow mountain roads. Access to the area was cutoff. In many places, there was no power or adequate food and water. There was also the danger of disease spreading from broken sewers and drains.

● Hungry earthquake survivors wait in line for food supplies from a Pakistani aid organization.

# Rescue Attempts

The army brought in helicopters to airlift supplies and to carry the injured to hospital. By November, more than 350,000 tents, 3.2 million blankets, and 3,300 tons (3,000 t) of medicines had been distributed. Tent villages were set up for those who had lost their homes. The numerous aftershocks made relief work dangerous. Progress in finding permanent shelter for the victims was slow. A year later, about 400,000 people faced a second freezing winter without permanent shelter in the mountains and valleys of northern Pakistan.

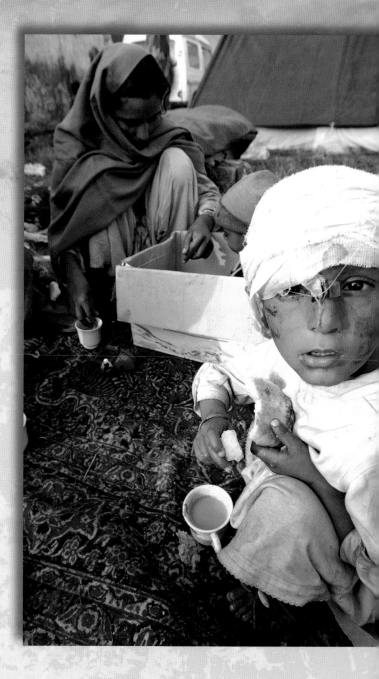

- Many children lost one or both of their parents.

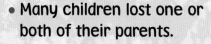

## DATA FILE

- The Pakistan earthquake was the most powerful earthquake in the region in over 100 years.

- More than 1,000 hospitals were destroyed.

- At least 69,000 people were severely injured, and 10,000 children were left disabled.

- More than 6,000 schools and colleges were destroyed.

- The northern Pakistan town of Balakot suffered the most damage. Rather than rebuild it in this dangerous location, the authorities moved the town to a new site just 14 miles (22 km) away.

# Why Do Earthquakes Happen?

The Earth's **crust** is made up of huge pieces called plates. These fit together like a giant jigsaw puzzle. Most earthquakes occur where these plates meet.

## A Moving Surface

The plates float on a layer of sticky **molten rock**. They move an average of about 2 inches (5 cm) a year. This is about the rate at which fingernails grow. But over millions of years, the plates move great distances. Sometimes, pressure builds up until the **rocks** bend, slip past each other, or split. This forms a crack called a **fault**. The movement causes the land above to shake violently. **Shock waves** move outward and upward from the starting point (or **focus**).

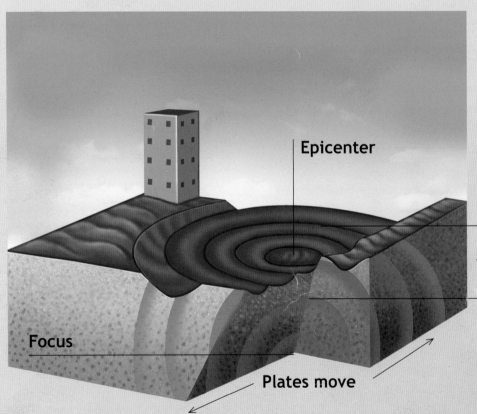

Epicenter

• Earthquakes occur when the edges of two of Earth's plates that are stuck together suddenly break free.

Vibrations reach the surface

Vibrations travel through rocks

Focus

Plates move

# Earthquake Zones

The Pacific Plate, beneath the Pacific Ocean, is the largest plate. Earthquakes and **volcanoes** occur all around the edges of the Pacific Plate. Another **earthquake zone** runs through the Mediterranean Sea and across southern Asia. The west coasts of North and South America and the middle of the Atlantic and Indian oceans are also at risk. Most of the joints between Earth's plates are under oceans and seas, but some, such as the plates that caused the Pakistan earthquake, are on land.

- **This map shows some of the main plates that make up Earth's crust.**

## DATA FILE

- Earth has seven major plates and many minor plates.

- Plates can move up to 5 inches (13 cm) a year.

- A plate traveling at 2 inches (5 cm) a year will travel about 31 miles (50 km) in a million years.

- Plates are 62 miles (100 km) thick.

- Plates can push into each other, pull away from each other, slide past each other, or one plate can slide on top of another.

- Most volcanoes and earthquakes occur where plates meet.

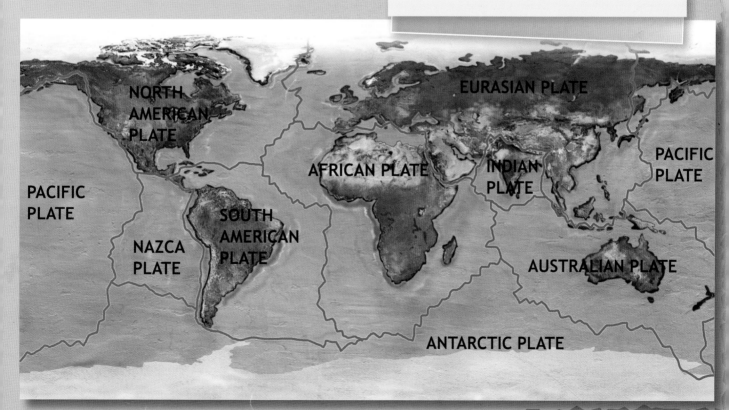

NORTH AMERICAN PLATE

EURASIAN PLATE

AFRICAN PLATE

INDIAN PLATE

PACIFIC PLATE

PACIFIC PLATE

NAZCA PLATE

SOUTH AMERICAN PLATE

AUSTRALIAN PLATE

ANTARCTIC PLATE

# Moving Cities

The people of California are used to living with the possibility of earthquakes. Their state is split north to south by a huge crack in Earth's surface called the **San Andreas Fault.**

## City Suburbs

The San Andreas Fault is found where the Pacific Plate moves northward, grating past the North American Plate. This movement is causing Los Angeles to move toward San Francisco at a rate of approximately 2 inches (5 cm) a year. At this rate, in about 15 million years, Los Angeles will be a suburb of San Francisco. Every year, there are about 20,000 minor **tremors** in the area. Occasionally, a more serious earthquake occurs.

• The San Andreas Fault runs along the western coast of the United States. It is one of the most unstable fault lines in the world.

# Rush-Hour Chaos

There was a disastrous earthquake in San Francisco in 1906 and another in 1989. On October 17, 1989, about 62,000 people were at game three of the World Series at the local stadium. At 5:04 P.M., a 25 mile (40 km) long crack opened in Earth's surface. Six seconds later, the shock waves reached San Francisco. Fortunately, although it was rush hour, the roads were less busy than usual. Many people were at the baseball game or watching the event on television. Even so, the earthquake, which measured 7.1 on the Richter scale, killed 68 people and caused $6 billion in damage.

## DATA FILE

- The 15-second earthquake caused damage up to 59 miles (95 km) from the **epicenter**.

- 18,306 homes and 2,575 businesses were damaged in the area close to the epicenter.

- 3,757 people were injured and 12,000 were left homeless.

- At the time, it was the most expensive natural disaster in U.S. history.

- The flexible Golden Gate Bridge remained standing, while more rigid bridges collapsed under the strain.

● In 1989, fire and gas explosions added to the dangers faced by the residents of San Francisco after a powerful earthquake.

**Date:** October 1989
**Location:** San Francisco
**Strength:** 7.1 on the Richter scale
**Fatalities:** 68

# Measuring Earthquakes

Only a few hundred earthquakes cause significant damage each year. Their power and effects are measured by **seismologists**. They record the strength of earthquakes using sensitive instruments.

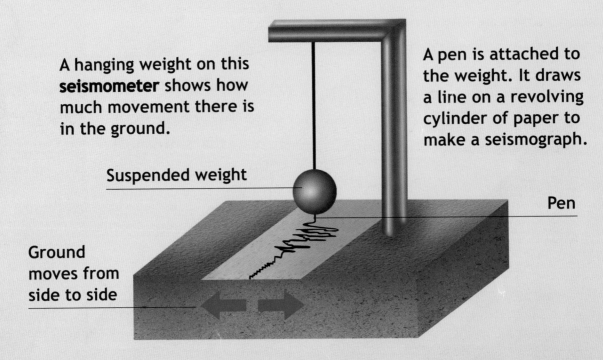

A hanging weight on this **seismometer** shows how much movement there is in the ground.

A pen is attached to the weight. It draws a line on a revolving cylinder of paper to make a seismograph.

Suspended weight

Pen

Ground moves from side to side

• A seismometer is used to measure earthquakes.

## The Richter Scale

When plates jerk against each other, energy is released into rocks nearby as shock waves. The Richter scale measures the strength of these waves. The scale is measured in steps—each successive unit is 10 times more powerful than the one before. Therefore, an earthquake that measures 7.0 on the Richter scale is 1,000 times more powerful than an earthquake measuring 4.0. Little damage is done by an earthquake below 4.0; an earthquake of 7.0, however, would cause great destruction.

# Comparing Earthquakes

The Richter scale allows us to compare the size of earthquakes, but it tells us little about their effect on human lives. An earthquake in Alaska in 1964, for example, measured 8.4 on the Richter scale and killed 131 people. In contrast, an earthquake in Morocco in 1960 measured 5.8 and killed up to 14,000 people. The most powerful and deadliest earthquakes occur nearest the surface, but other factors affect the death toll, too. The time of day, the population of the area, and the number of buildings are also important factors.

- The damage caused by an earthquake depends on how deep the tremors occur.

# Populated Areas

Turkey has a long history of earthquakes. Virtually the entire country is situated on a small plate that is squeezed between three larger plates with frequent disastrous results.

## Squeezed Between Plates

The Turkish Plate is being squeezed between the Eurasian Plate to the north and the African Plate and Arabian Plate to the south. It moves sideways to the west at a rate of .39–7.9 inches (1–20 cm) a year. In 1999, this movement caused a powerful earthquake close to the city of Izmit.

● These apartments in Izmit collapsed during the earthquake.

**Date:** August 1999
**Location:** Northwest Turkey
**Strength:** 7.4 on the Richter scale
**Fatalities:** Up to 45,000

# Spectacular Fire

Unfortunately, the area where the earthquake occurred is the most densely populated part of Turkey. It is also heavily industrialized with an oil refinery, car factories, and the headquarters of the Turkish Navy. One of the effects of the earthquake was the collapse of a tower at an oil refinery. This started a fire in an area where 771,610 tons (700,000 t) of oil were stored. It took firefighters several days to bring the blaze under control.

## News Flash

August 17, 1999

As rescue workers fought desperately through the night to free victims from twisted concrete and steel, shocked survivors of the earthquake in northwestern Turkey struggled to come to terms with the scope of devastation and human loss. Officials said more than 2,000 people were already dead.

- The 1999 earthquake caused a huge fire at this oil refinery in northwest Turkey.

# Rebuilding Lives

Thousands of homes and businesses were damaged or destroyed. The earthquake caused 17,127 deaths and 43,953 people were injured. The number of deaths was probably much greater than this, however—perhaps as high as 45,000. No one knows for sure because the bodies were quickly buried to prevent the spread of disease. The death toll increased the following winter because survivors were living in poor conditions—in tents or makeshift shelters on the streets.

- The 1999 earthquake sent this bus and these buildings tumbling into the Sea of Marmara in Turkey.

- While many modern buildings collapsed during the earthquake, older buildings, such as this mosque, were virtually undamaged.

## Learning Lessons

The area was studied by scientists immediately after the earthquake. They found that most of the deaths and injuries were caused by collapsed office and apartment buildings, usually four to eight stories high and made of reinforced concrete. Hundreds of buildings that had covered the fault collapsed because their **foundations** were torn apart. The soft, wet soil covering much of the area had caused many other buildings to sink when the earthquake struck. The ground north of the fault had also dropped 6 feet (2 m) below the ground south of the fault.

### DATA FILE

- The Izmit, Turkey, earthquake lasted 37 seconds.

- More than 250,000 people lost their homes.

- The first of many aftershocks occurred just 20 minutes after the original earthquake.

- The earthquake produced a tsunami within the enclosed Sea of Marmara.

- Five men, trapped in the basement of a collapsed building, managed to call the rescuers on a cell phone. They were pulled out—bruised and dirty, but alive!

# Earthquakes at Sea

On December 26, 2004, there was a powerful earthquake off the coast of Indonesia. It triggered a deadly series of waves, called a tsunami, that killed about 280,000 people and destroyed millions of homes and livelihoods.

**Date:** December 2004
**Location:** Countries bordering the Indian Ocean
**Strength:** 9.2 on the Richter scale
**Fatalities:** 280,000

## The Longest Earthquake

The earthquake occurred near the island of Sumatra in the Indian Ocean. It measured 9.2 on the Richter scale and lasted for almost 10 minutes, making it the longest earthquake on record. As Earth's plates jerked violently apart, they slid up to 59 feet (18 m) in a few minutes.

• During the 2004 tsunami, a series of giant waves destroyed the city of Banda Aceh in Sumatra.

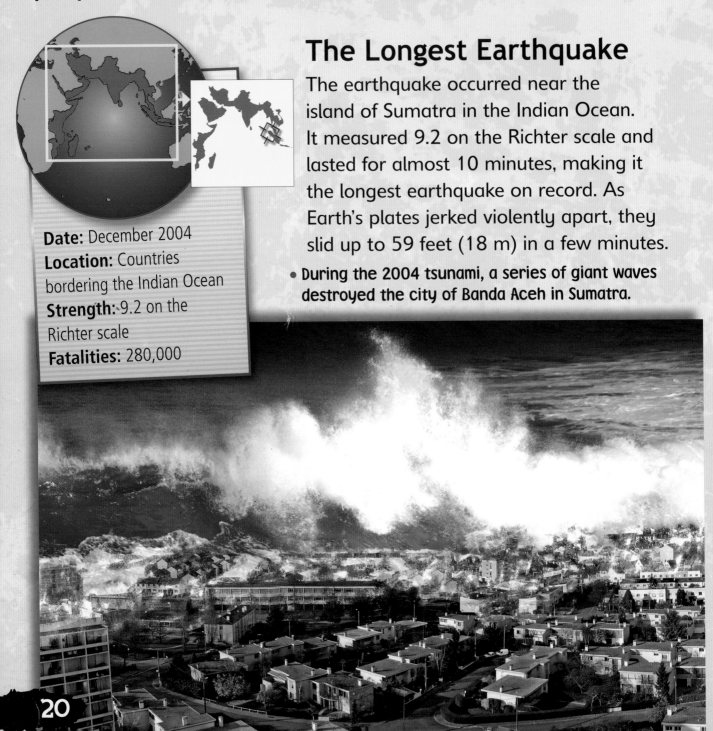

# Energy Release

The earthquake's energy was enough to make Earth wobble on its **axis** by up to 1 inch (2.5 cm). The sea floor along the fault line was forced upward by more than 15 feet (4.5 m). This moved 7 cubic miles (30 cubic km) of sea water with a great deal of energy. Waves began to spread out through the ocean away from the epicenter of the earthquake —this was a tsunami.

## News Flash
December 31, 2004

The death toll from Sunday's tsunami has jumped to more than 118,000 after it was reported that nearly 80,000 people were killed in Indonesia alone. Estimates of the death toll continue to rise in most other areas.

• This fishing boat was thrown onto the roof of a house by the 100 foot (30 m) high waves pushed up by the tsunami.

• This aerial photograph shows how huge waves devastated the coastal towns of Indonesia in the 2004 tsunami.

## Ripples in the Ocean

By chance, two satellites were passing over the Indian Ocean as the earthquake struck. This provided an accurate picture of what happened. At first, the waves were mere ripples. Ships passed over them without those on board noticing anything was wrong. But close to the shore, the waves slowed and grew to a great height. Coastal areas had almost no warning of the approaching tsunami. The only warning came just before the first wave struck when the sea suddenly retreated from the shore, exposing hundreds of feet of seabed.

# Disaster Strikes

The waves of the tsunami struck the coast at intervals of up to 40 minutes. The tsunami traveled 2,800 miles (4,500 km) from the coast of Indonesia to Somalia in East Africa in just 7 hours. The waves had tremendous energy, stripping sand from beaches, tearing up trees, and destroying towns and villages. About 280,000 local people and tourists were killed or listed as missing and presumed dead. The tsunami caused more casualties than any other in recorded history.

- Rescue workers search for survivors in the wreckage left by the 2004 tsunami.

## DATA FILE

- The 2004 tsunami was one of the deadliest natural disasters.

- It killed about 280,000 people and affected 14 countries.

- Indonesia, Sri Lanka, India, and Thailand were hit hardest, but the tsunami caused serious damage as far away as East Africa.

- The energy released by the earthquake that triggered the tsunami was equal to 23,000 atomic bombs.

- There was no tsunami warning system in place to warn people of the approaching danger.

# Walls of Water

A tsunami is produced when an earthquake, volcano, or even a meteorite shakes the seabed. This jolt causes a series of waves to form.

## Growing Waves

As the seabed moves, it causes the water to rise and form a series of waves. The waves travel in all directions from the area of disturbance, much like the ripples formed when a pebble is thrown into a pond. At first, the waves are less than 1.6 feet (0.5 m) high and look similar to ordinary waves. But as they approach the shallow waters along the coast, the friction of the seabed acts like a brake, forcing the waves to slow down dramatically. As they do so, the waves grow to a great height. This wall of water, sometimes over 100 feet (30 m) high, causes massive destruction along the coast.

- When a tsunami forms, the movement of Earth's plates (1) creates a series of waves that travel across the ocean (2 and 3) and grow enormously as they reach the shallow coastline (4).

1
Earthquake

2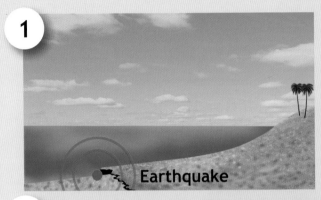
Water moves

3
Waves travel across ocean

4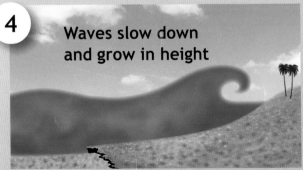
Waves slow down and grow in height

# Deadly Approach

Tsunamis are often mistakenly called tidal waves, but they have nothing to do with the tides. Tsunami waves are dangerous because of their strength and speed. They move across the ocean at rates of up to 500 miles (800 km) per hour. A tsunami caused by an earthquake in Los Angeles, for example, could reach Tokyo, Japan, quicker than a jet airliner could fly between the two cities. The lack of warning means that people and animals may be unable to retreat to safety.

- Special buoys now form a chain across the oceans to give early warning of an approaching tsunami.

## DATA FILE

- Normal ocean waves are caused by the wind blowing across the surface and whipping the water into ripples.

- The first tsunami observation stations were built across the Pacific Ocean (where most tsunamis occur) to warn of approaching waves.

- Hawaii is the state with the greatest number of tsunamis (about one a year—serious damage occurs about once every seven years).

- Most tsunamis come in a series of a dozen waves or more with 5–60 minutes between them.

# Man-Made Tremors

Anything that puts Earth's crust under pressure can trigger an earthquake. Some people believe that certain human activities may cause earthquakes now or in the future.

## Rocks Under Pressure

Evidence suggests that large man-made dams and reservoirs put huge pressure on the surrounding rocks. If the pressure causes these rocks to move, they could trigger an earthquake. In 1967, for example, an earthquake measuring 6.5 on the Richter scale hit Koyna, India, shortly after a new reservoir had been built. Other earthquakes across the world have been linked to the testing of nuclear weapons, mining, quarrying, and oil and gas production.

● The construction of large dams and reservoirs can put pressure on the rocks below.

## Melting Ice

Scientists believe a powerful earthquake occurred in Sweden about 8,500 years ago, although the area is far from plate boundaries. The entire region was emerging from the last Ice Age and had been covered with thick ice that pushed the land down for many feet. But when the ice melted, the land sprang back to its original height along lines of weakness. It is possible that we are creating the conditions for similar earthquakes in the future. These earthquakes could occur because of the effects of **global warming**.

• Glaciers and ice caps are beginning to melt because of global warming. This could cause future earthquakes.

# Reduced Impact

It is not earthquakes that kill people—it is buildings!
One way to reduce the impact of earthquakes is to
make buildings that can withstand the violent shaking
that occurs during an earthquake.

## Solid Foundations

Two earthquakes, each 6.5 on
the Richter, struck in December
2003. The one in California killed
two people; the other, in Bam,
Iran, killed 26,000. The difference
was mostly due to the types of
buildings in each city. Today,
new houses and offices in many
earthquake zones are built on
solid rocks with a framework
of strong flexible steel. Although
San Francisco has many
earthquakes, its tallest building,
the Transamerica Pyramid
building, is 846 feet (258 m)
high. It has deep foundations.
Its tapered shape makes it less
likely to topple. During the
1989 earthquake, the top of the
building swayed by as much as
12 inches (30 cm), but the
building did not collapse.

• Because of its design, the Transamerica
Pyramid building was able to withstand
the tremors of an earthquake.

# Shock Absorbers

The Torre Mayor building in Mexico City is 738 feet (225 m) tall. Its deep foundations reach down 130 feet (40 m) to hard rock and are designed to move with an earthquake. It is also fitted with huge **shock absorbers** that soak up vibrations.

- The Torre Mayor building is designed to bend slightly during an earthquake.

## DATA FILE

To keep safe during an earthquake:

- If you are indoors, take cover under a sturdy desk or table and make yourself small with knees on the floor and head tucked down toward the floor.

- Keep away from windows, fireplaces, stoves, and heavy items, such as television sets, that might topple over.

- Make sure you know how to turn off the gas supply where you live.

- Make sure you know where the fire extinguishers are and how to use them.

- If you are outdoors, stay away from buildings and power lines.

# Glossary

**aftershock** an earthquake that occurs after the original or main earthquake

**axis** an imaginary line around which an object, such as Earth, can spin or rotate

**crust** Earth's outer layer of rock on which we live

**earthquake** a violent shaking of the ground caused by Earth's plates moving

**earthquake zone** a region where earthquakes occur in clusters

**epicenter** the point on Earth's crust that lies immediately above the focus of an earthquake

**fault** a large crack or break in a series of rocks; the rocks on one, or both sides, of the fault may slip up or down

**focus** the point underground where rocks break during an earthquake

**foundation** the solid base on which a building is constructed

**global warming** the warming of Earth's atmosphere as a result of polluting gases, such as carbon dioxide and methane

**landslide** a large quantity of rock or soil falling or sliding very quickly down a slope

**molten rock** the hot, liquid rock found just below Earth's crust

**plate** a section of Earth's crust; the slow, steady movements of the plates cause changes in Earth's surface

**Richter scale** a scale used to measure and compare the strengths of earthquakes

**rock** the solid part of Earth's crust beneath the soil

**San Andreas Fault** a huge crack in Earth's crust that runs along much of the western coast of the United States; many earthquakes occur along this faultline

**seismologist** a scientist who studies earthquakes

**seismometer** an instrument used to measure and record ground movements

**shock absorber** a device that reduces the effect of knocks, jolts, or vibrations

**shock waves** the movements created at the focus of an earthquake

**subcontinent** a major subdivision of a continent

**tremor** a shaking or vibration of the ground

**tsunami** a series of large sea waves, usually caused by an earthquake near the seabed

**vibration** the action of moving quickly to and fro, or up and down

**volcano** a hole or tear in Earth's crust from which molten rock (lava) flows

# Index

# Web Sites

www.fema.gov/hazard/earthquake
Find information and advice about what to do in an earthquake.

http://earthquake.usgs.gov/learning/kids
Learn facts about earthquakes.

www.nationalgeographic.com/ngkids/0403/main.html
This site provides an interactive introduction to earthquakes.

www.weatherwizkids.com/earthquake1.htm
This site provides an introduction to earthquakes and tsunamis and includes animations.

http://www.nationalgeographic.com/ngkids/9610/kwave/
This site provides an introduction to tsunamis.